HEATHER RAFFO'S
9 PARTS OF DESIRE

HEATHER RAFFO'S

9 PARTS
OF DESIRE

A Play

Northwestern University Press
Evanston, Illinois

Northwestern University Press
www.nupress.northwestern.edu

Printed in the United States of America

10 9 8 7 6 5 4 3 2 1

ISBN 0-8101-2345-2 (paper)
ISBN 0-8101-2416-5 (paper with CD)

Special thanks to Geraldine Brooks for the inspiration of her book *Nine Parts of Desire*

Translation of Arabic words and "The Well" by Sinan Antoon
Translation of "Che Mali Wali" by Salaam Yousif

Cover and interior production photographs copyright © Irene Young; last two interior photographs of set design by Antje Ellermann
Front cover: Mullaya

Library of Congress Cataloging-in-Publication data are available from the Library of Congress.

♾ The paper used in this publication meets the minimum requirements of the American National Standard for Information Sciences—Permanence of Paper for Printed Library Materials, ANSI z39.48-1992.

*God created sexual desire in ten parts;
then he gave nine parts to women
and one to men.*

    —Ali b. Abi Talib, fourth caliph after Muhammad. Revered
    as the founder of the Shi`a sect of Islam, his shrine is in
    Najaf, Iraq, and is a major place of Shi`a pilgrimage.

CONTENTS

This play was inspired by a life changing trip I made to Iraq in 1993. It was only a few years after the Gulf War had ended, and I was longing to see my family. To my childhood memory Baghdad was the magical place I had been as a little girl and where I'd slept on the roof of my grandmother's house under the stars. But since the gut-wrenching war, Baghdad was simply where more than fifty of my immediate relatives still lived.

It would be my first time back to Iraq as an adult. The only way into Iraq at this time was by bus across the desert, for me a seventeen-hour trip in total from Amman, Jordan. When I reached the Iraqi border, everyone from my bus got into the line for Middle Easterners except me. To them I was classified as "other," so I had to go down a long hallway into a back room. There was a man behind a desk; he opened my passport, looked at me, then back down at the passport. He got up, walked all the way across the room, and shook my hand. He said, "Welcome to your father's country, we hope you take back a good impression of the Iraqi people, know our people are not our government, please be at home here, and when you return tell your people about us."

Seven hours later I was in Baghdad, hugging all fifty members of my father's family. They called me their daughter; they fought over who would cook me dinner and whose house I would visit first. I was like an orphan finding her family on that trip, soaking up every story about their lives and how my father grew up. I saw buildings my grandfather and great-grandfather had carved from marble; I saw the house my father grew up in; and I saw the obvious destruction of the country. Across the street from my uncle's house was a pile of rubble, a neighbor's house and a casualty of a stray bomb.

I visited the Amiriyya bomb shelter where many Iraqi civilians lost their lives when the shelter became a target in the 1991 war. I went to the Saddam Art Center, the modern art museum of Baghdad, and saw room after room of billboard-sized portraits of Saddam Hussein. Then I wandered into a small room and there was a haunting painting of a nude woman clinging to a barren tree. Her head was hanging, bowed, and there was a golden light behind her, like a sun. The painting was titled *Savagery*.

This painting lived with me for many years, haunting me and tugging at me to tell its story. I began by researching the artist. She had been killed by an American air raid in June of 1993, a few months before I saw her painting hanging in the Saddam Art Center. It was a national tragedy, a beloved female artist and curator of the museum, killed by an American bomb. I knew I would never meet her, but I wanted to talk to other Iraqi artists who were her contemporaries. One by one I was introduced to Iraqi women who had lived through more than I could imagine. Along the way *9 Parts of Desire* would come to include a multitude of Iraqis' stories. They shared so deeply of themselves and seemed to tell me almost anything, but only after I shared as much of myself with them. My process was not one of formal interviews but rather a process of spending time together living, eating, communicating compassionately, and loving on such a level that when I parted from their homes it was clear to all that we were now family. When an Iraqi woman trusts you, it is because she has come to love you, and that has been the process of finding and forming these stories.

With rare exception, these stories are not told verbatim. Most are composites, and although each character is based on research, I consider all the women in my play to be dramatized characters in a poetic story. I liken it to songwriting—I listened deeply to what each woman said, what she wanted to say but couldn't, and what she never knew how to say. Then I wrote her song.

PRODUCTION HISTORY

Heather Raffo's 9 Parts of Desire was first developed with VoiceChair Productions under the direction and dramaturgy of Eva Breneman. Its initial production was at the Traverse Theatre, Edinburgh, in August 2003, and it later moved to the Bush Theatre in London, where it was repeatedly chosen as one of the "Five Best Plays" in London by *The Independent*. The play was next developed as part of the Immigrant Voices Project in January 2004 at Queens Theatre in the Park under the direction of Jack Hofsiss.

In May 2004 the Public Theatre, New York, selected it to be part of their New Work Now festival of readings where it developed further under the direction of Kate Saxon.

This version of *9 Parts of Desire* had its New York premiere in October 2004 at the Manhattan Ensemble Theatre, with producer David Fishelson and under the direction of Joanna Settle. It won the 2005 Blackburn Prize Special Commendation, the Marian Seldes–Garson Kanin Fellowship, as well as the 2005 Lucille Lortel Award for best solo show and best sound design. It ran for nine months, had five extensions, and was a critic's pick (of the *New York Times*, *Time Out*, and *Village Voice*) for more than twenty-four weeks in a row.

Cast	Heather Raffo
Director	Joanna Settle
Sound design	Obadiah Eaves
Set design	Antje Ellermann
Lighting design	Peter West
Costume design	Mattie Ullrich
Properties	Kathy Fabian
Creative consultant	Morgan Jenness
Production stage manager	Lisa Gavaletz

Costume design for the Geffen Theater, Los Angeles, and touring productions as seen in the photographs of this publication are by Kasia Walicka Maimone.

HEATHER RAFFO'S
9 PARTS OF DESIRE

For my family in Iraq

CHARACTER LIST

Mullaya

Layal

Amal

Huda

The Doctor

Iraqi Girl

Umm Ghada

The American

Nanna

Throughout the play the woman uses an abaya, *a traditional black robelike garment, to move from character to character. Some characters wear the* abaya *traditionally; others use it as a prop. The Arabic words* aa *(yes) and* la *(no) are used throughout. Iraqi terms and lyrics to the songs can be found in the glossary (see page 73).*

[*The first sound we hear is the dawn call to prayer. In Muslim countries the call to prayer is heard five times a day: at dawn, at midday, in the afternoon, at sunset, and finally when the sky becomes dark and daytime is over. The call to prayer is heard five times in the course of this play. The* MULLAYA *walks onstage singing "Che Mali Wali," a traditional Iraqi song. She carries a great bundle on her head. She empties her load of shoes into the river. Traditionally, a* MULLAYA *is a woman in Arabic culture hired to lead call-and-response with women mourning at funerals. She is considered very good if she can bring the women to a crying frenzy with her improvised, heartbreaking verses about the dead. Mythic, celebratory, and inviting, this* MULLAYA's *mourning is part of her ritual ablutions.*]

MULLAYA:
Early in the morning
I come to throw dead shoes into the river

without this river there would be no here
there would be no beginning
it is why I come.

Take off your slippers
take off your sandals
take off your boots

appease the hungry
so I can sleep beneath the stars without fear
of being consumed
or

the river again will flood
the river again will be damned
the river again will be diverted
today the river must eat.

When the grandson of Genghis Khan
burned all the books in Baghdad
the river ran black with ink.
What color is this river now?
It runs the color of old shoes
the color of distances
the color of soles torn and worn
this river is the color of worn soles.

This land between two rivers
I only see the one—
where is the other river
more circular and slow?
Why only this one straight and fast?
Where is the other?
And the other land?
Where is anything they said there would be?
We were promised so much
the Garden of—

Let me tell you I have walked across it
Qurna, Eridu, Ur
the Garden of Eden was here

its roots and its rivers
and before this Garden
the chaos and the fighting
loud and angry children—
the dark sea lies beneath my country still
as it has always done
sweet and bitter water—children of Nammu.
But our marshlands now are different
they've been diverted, dammed, and dried
I have walked from there to here
from the flood
to the highway of death
collecting, carrying
you can read the story
here it is, read it all here
on my sole.

My feet hurt
I have holes in my shoes
I have holes now even in my feet
there are holes everywhere
even in this story.

I don't want new shoes!
I would rather swim than walk—
bring me back the water I was created in
the water in which I woke each morning
and went to bed each night
the water in which I swam to school
and milked the buffalo
and listened to the loud voices of frogs
bring me back the marshes and the fishes
reed man, reed woman

I would rather swim than walk—
and now the river has developed an appetite for us
its current runs back
beneath Iraq
to where Apsu and Tiamat are cradling still
underneath my country
there is no paradise of martyrs
only water
a great dark sea
of desire
and I will feed it
my worn sole.

[LAYAL, *an artist, wears the* abaya *loosely hanging off her shoulders like a dressing gown or painting smock.* LAYAL *is sexy and elegant, a resilient and fragile woman. She is a daredevil with a killer smile.*]

LAYAL:
Leave Iraq?

[*She giggles oddly as she tries to imagine it.*]

Well, I could move I suppose—

My sister wants me to come to London
she has a house and an art studio there now—
I could go I have the money.

I don't know
maybe I feel guilty
all of us here
it's a shame if all the artists leave too—
who will be left to inspire the people if all the

artists and intellectuals run?
Most of them already have
my sister included.

I don't judge
I mean for most
they feel they cannot express themselves
because always it is life and death—
even I should have been dead twice before I tell you
but I'm not
death is only teasing me. [*She laughs.*]
Maybe that's it, maybe I stay because
I feel lucky, I am charmed, what can touch me?

Besides what's to paint outside Iraq?
Maybe I am not so good artist outside Iraq—

Here my work is well known.
Hardly anyone will paint nudes anyway
but this is us
our bodies—isn't it?
Deserted
in a void
and we are looking for something always
I think it's light.

Always I am fighting to keep
transparency
because once it goes muddy I can't get it back.
It's not oil, with oil you just paint over what you've done
with oil, light it's the last thing you add
but with watercolor, white
is the space you leave empty from the beginning.

I think I help people maybe
to be transcending
but secretly.
Always I paint them as me
or as trees sometimes like I was telling you.
I do not ever want to expose exactly another woman's body
so I paint my body
but her body, herself inside me.
So it is not me alone
it is all of us
but I am the body that takes the experience.
Your experience, yourself, I will take it
only you and I will know who it is
and the others let them say
oh Layal, again she is obsessed with her body! [*She laughs.*]

I did a painting once of a woman
eaten by Saddam's son
that's how I describe it.
A beautiful young student, from University of Baghdad—
Uday he asked her out, and she couldn't refuse,
he took her and beat her brutally, like is his way—
and she went back to campus and
her roommate saw the bruises and things and asked her
"What happened?"
And she so stupid, innocent girl told her the truth.
Why she talks such things?
Iraqis they know not to open their mouth not even for the dentist.
Of course Uday, he took her back
with his friends, they
stripped her
covered her in honey
and watched his Dobermans eat her.

See in my painting she is the branch's blossom
leaning over the barking dogs
they cannot reach
no matter how hungry they are
not unless they learn to climb her
but they are dogs, they never will.

You see, nobody knows the painting is her
but I believe somewhere she sees.

That is me, [*laughing*] my philosophy!
These stories are living inside of me
each woman I meet her or I hear about her
and I cannot separate myself from them
I am so compassionate to them, so attached—*la, la,* it's the opposite
maybe I do feel separate, so separate from the women here
I am always trying to be part of them.
I feel I could have been anybody if I looked different—

Some other artists more senior than myself
would have hoped to be curator of Saddam Art Center
these jobs they are hard to come by and
it takes a lot to get them.
Always they make a rumor of me
that I got this position because I was having an affair
at that time they said
with Saddam's cousin—
they can believe what they like
I don't care what people say.
Anyway he's dead now of course
this cousin
a mysterious plane crash
you see.

If—
If I'd had an affair with him
how would that have made my life any easier?
Isn't everything in this country a matter of survival?
I don't care if you are with the government
or a prisoner of it.
Even loving
just the simple act of loving
can make you suffer so deeply.

So if I am now in a position of grace, favor, rumor
so be it
I don't care
I am still trying
to be revealing something
in my trees, my nudes, my portraits of Saddam—

I fear it here
and I love it here
I cannot stop what I am here
I am obsessed by it
by these things that we all are but we are not saying.
"Either I shall die"—how does it go?
Oh my favorite, Shahrazad! [*An aching giggle.*] "Either I shall die
or I shall live a ransom for all the virgin daughters of Muslims
and the cause of their deliverance from his hands to life!"

Well, I am not a person of great sacrifice
I have sacrificed in my life, sure,
but nothing like what I see around me.
Anyway that is life. You cannot compare, only be compassionate.
I try to have understanding of all sides, and I have compassion
just not enough.

I'm a good artist.

I'm an OK mother.

I'm a miserable wife.

I've loved yes, many
but
not enough.

But I am good at being naked
that's what I do, in secret.

[*Bright, festive, and robust,* AMAL *is a woman of thirty-eight who looks so intently at whomever she is talking to you would swear her eyes never blinked. She asks many questions; she really thinks there is an answer out there for her.* AMAL *wears the* abaya *fastened behind her head and flowing voluptuously about her body.*]

AMAL:
I see with my heart
not with my eyes.
I am Bedouin
I cannot tell you if a man is fat or if a man is handsome
only I can tell you if I love this man or not.
And I think you see with your heart like a Bedouin.

I do, I very much feel this void
and I have no peace
always I am looking for peace.
Do you know peace?
I think only mens have real peace
womans she cannot have peace
what you think?

My mother when I come home she is so happy to see me,
she sing to me
she sing, "Amal my beautiful girl
Amal whose hair is black like night
Amal whose eyes are black like deep coal
Amal my daughter whose body is strong for her love"—
and my voice, I have to sing to my mother, "I am home again!"
But never I think I am different
we in our village we believe our mothers.
I have *tis`ah*—nine brothers and five sisters—
and nobody make me feel fat.
But I learn now I am big.
So don't you think I am fat?
La, la, I am very big
but I am diet now and my childrens too
both they are diet.
Aa, aa I have two childrens
fourteen and eight.

My husband, first husband, he was Saudi,
he is now in London
on this big road they call it
where all the big plastic surgeons are.

Aa, aa, I was there with him
I like London very much
I study there
I like to
walk with my friends in this Portobello market and—

I left him.
I was feeding my daughter, Tala, at the time

and driving my son Omar to school
I forgot some papers for Omar
so I drove back home to get them
and I saw my husband in bed with my very close friend
and really I am shock
because he is Bedouin,
but Saudi Bedouin.
And even he would say to me when I talked,
during our relations,
he'd say, "Don't say these things they are dirty things."
I wanted to enjoy myself with him
but he—
and then he goes and—

So
I didn't say anything
I told a friend
go into my house
and get my passport and the children's passport
and I left
I never told him why I left.

I came back to Iraq
but I didn't like to live in our town
it's too small, I don't feel free even
always my brothers looking out for me I feel too much closed
and so I come—
not here, *la*, I—

I went to Israel first.

You see, our very close tribesman came to visit
because my father he is the sheikh.

This tribesman, he is of the same Bedouin tribe as me
but born Israeli—
and always when I was a girl I thinking
oh to marry one from my tribe
we have the same accent, same eyes, same nature, very big heart!
This tribesman he never feel the woman his enemy
he feel sorry for her and feel only to keep her happy
and the woman she feels him very man—
we are very special together
so I marry him, my second marriage,
and I went to his village in Israel.

He promise me
we would move and go to Europe somewheres or Canada
but then we never move
his wife didn't want—
aa, his other wife, number one, she makes him stay.
He would have taken both of us
it could have been good
but she was crazy
really she was, I think they fight a lot.
Number one, she would leave him to go to her father's house
for six months at a time and I taking care of her eight childs.
I mother one of her childs
I fed her son—oh Koran, you must know it—
if you feed for more than seven days, full feeding,
that child is like your child
and this child must never marry with your child
because now they are brother and sister in the milk
so it is *haram*, sin,
because they have your blood inside them both.
But wife, number one, she was very skinny, not well
she would go away for such a long times—

we couldn't live together like this
he is very jealousy man, very Bedouin
and I am looking for this freedom
and he says "No, we are not going to Canada."
So I care very much for him, but again
I left.

I come back to Iraq with my children
but to Baghdad to be in city.
I come here, and my family don't like
they don't support me but—

I got some money.
I got some money from a friend of
my first ex-husband, his name's Sa`ad.
And we start to talk on the phone, this friend, Sa`ad,
he is in London, and me here. We talk for one year.
I talk to him honest, I am very honest person
I told him exactly I am thirty-eight, and this is how I look.
I hide nothing from him
I told him everything in my heart
everything I hope and
I felt peace.
It is beautiful to talk so much
because he
he tells me from inside himself too
very deep, very sincere
for one year.
I felt safe the first time in my life
I felt myself with this man and
I love him! [*She laughs.*]

We talk and we say we will get married, third marriage, oh!
He says let us meet in Dubai
because the war it was then and if he comes back home to Iraq
they may keep him.

So I left my job, I left everything.
I telephone to his family congratulations
he telephone to my family
and we go to meet in this hotel in Dubai
we go to dinner
he says after dinner
"I am going I will call you later"
and I waiting in my hotel room so happy to see this man I love.
I telephone hims at two A.M. and he says, "No, not now
I am drunk"—
I say, "Let us talk I want to talk
we spent one year on the phone talking everything
finally we see each other
my heart is so full to share"—
he says, "No Amal,
no," he says, "it is over
do not talk to me anymore."
I am crying really I don't understand what he means
but he say,
"You are too pure for me
what you do with a man like me?
I am twenty year older than you
soon I will be very olds man and you will have to take care of me
you are too good, too innocent for me."
I don't understand hims say this thing because I love him,
and he says, "No,"
"No," he says,
"you are not the Amal I love."

What does this mean?
I am not the Amal he love?

How he say this?
Why can this be?

I am shamed to my family
they think he slept with me that night
we meet in Dubai
and change his mind.

I don't have peace.

Always I am asking myself what he think of me?
What he seed in me that change him?
I see now I am fat.
Now I look for the first time to dress myself more pretty
I am doing my hair this way—
but I don't see hims fat, I don't see hims old
I see hims with my heart not with my eyes
and never have I love a man this much.
Even I love him.
Even.

My ex-husband, first one,
got us passports to bring the children to London
so they will see their father on the weekends
and have their schooling there
la, la, I think I told you this already.
But always I am thinking what if I run into Sa`ad when I go there
I would shake with all of me on my face
I don't know I can hide it
I will have my freedom there

but not my peace
maybe freedom is the better than peace?

—

I have never talked this before
nobody here knows this thing about me
I keep it in my heart only
oh, I talk a lot!

I wish to be like this! [*She laughs.*]

I want to be like you
this is the most free moment of my life
really I mean this
oh really I love you, like a sister I love you
the most free moment of my life.
Don't leave, stay with me
oh I need to talk every day this way.
Is this American way?
Tell me what you think
what should I do?
I want to memorize what you say,
so I can be this way freedom again.

But what do think he means, I am not the Amal he love?

[*A whiskey drinker with fifty years as a smoker,* HUDA *is an Iraqi exile in her seventies now living in London. She has a keen sense of humor.*]

HUDA:
Well exile in London for the intellectuals
is mostly scotch, of course politics, and poetry

it used to be Gauloises too but I have given up smoking—well—
Anyway, I tell you our dilemma,
some in the opposition praise America one hundred percent
they know they are the only power
and the whole policy of the world is in their hands.
Personally, I have my doubts about American policy,
still I prefer chaos to permanent repression and cruelty
because Saddam was the worst enemy to the people
than anybody else.

He beheaded seventy women for being prostitutes,
but he made them prostitutes.
Saddam's stooges, they'd kidnap a woman
just going from her car to her house,
and take her as a slave, sex slave
or house slave when they were in their hideouts,
and when they'd finish with her
he would go to her family saying "She is a prostitute"
and he'd behead her and put her head in the street.
There was no law if you are a prostitute you are beheaded.
So, what chaos is worse than this?
Let it be chaos at least something will come out of it.
Maybe it's the only way
but I am
for the war.

I didn't go to that antiwar march, *la*
in London alone they said there was what, *ya`ni,*
one million, two million in Hyde Park?
I couldn't march with anyone who was pro-Saddam.
I protested all my life, I was always political
even if I was bourgeois—
in '58 anybody who was intelligent was Communist.

When I lived in Beirut during their war I protested too,
everywhere I go there is a war.

[*She laughs and hacks.*]

I walked for peace in Vietnam,
I walked for Chile,
but this war it was personal, this war was against all my beliefs
and yet I wanted it.
Because Saddam
Saddam was the greater enemy than, I mean,
imperialism—

[*Nauseated,* THE DOCTOR *throws up. She washes her hands, then dries them on the* abaya. *Throughout, she is desperate to keep her hands clean. Exhausted, she clings to the factual.*]

THE DOCTOR:
I'm sorry, it's probably just the smell of the sewage backing up in the ward. I feel fine, fine, let's go on, it's just, it's so hot and the smell of it makes me—

[*She yells offstage.*]

Would somebody come clean this shit up before I slip in it!

Damn it! I lost her, the baby should be dead, not her. God she had enough, she had three girls at home, but she insisted, hoping for a boy. What am I supposed to tell her husband? Here, it's your firstborn son, I'm sorry he has two heads?

More than ultrasound, incubators, Panadol, anything, I need some—who can I ask? Look, just this month, I'll tell you, I've started counting:

six babies no head, four abnormally large heads, now today another one with two heads. Such high levels of genetic damage does not occur naturally. These things you see them in textbooks.

And the cancers, *la*, I've never seen them before in Iraq, girls of seven, eight years old with breast cancer. I told this girl, ten years old, she came in, she thought her breasts were developing but it was only on one side. It was the cancer. I told her it's OK, you can be like me, see how strong I am, I had breast cancer. She said, "I want to see it," so I showed her my scar, she hugged me. She thought she was developing. But it's toddlers even with breast cancer, more than one cancer in the same patient, whole families all suffering from cancer—

And what can stop it? I mean the children, they play at the sites even when they're fenced off, they take the bullets to school to show their classmates what they collected from America. One came in wearing a bullet around his neck—a bullet tipped in depleted uranium around his neck.

Especially here in Basra it's in the Shatt al-Arab, so it's in all the water, it's in the food, but if it's airborne like they say—haven't you noticed something? It could be depleted uranium, or chemicals that were released from the bombings during the Gulf War, but I can see something changed the environment—giant squash, huge tomatoes. They say the radiation in plants now is at eighty-four times the safety limit. But who can clean it? Ever? We will have this depleted uranium for what—four thousand years? How many generations is that growing up handicapped? I am afraid to see them when they're grown.

It's better, maybe, death—

My husband says death is worse, *il-mawt yihrig il-glub*, death burns the heart. But I don't believe—

Most of our men are already deformed from the wars. My husband he sits at home without his legs. He can't make money sitting at home, what's left of the man, I can't even look at him now, he's my death sentence. I don't care, honestly I don't care what I say. I'm a little ashamed of myself but it sickens me. We won't survive it, I won't, I'm a doctor, if I can't do anything. I trained in England, we all trained in the West, I could have been anywhere, I came back, you know what I'm talking about, we had the best hospitals in the Middle East, everyone was coming to us, and what are we now? We're the experiment.

Look at us
look at us—
wayn Allah, wayn Allah?

[*She is nauseated again.*]

No I'm fine, I'm fine
I'm pregnant.

[*The* IRAQI GIRL *plays with the* abaya, *wrapping it about her head like long luxurious hair and other times bundling it up to be her baby doll. However, we first catch her dancing with great abandon in her living room to something similar to N'Sync on her new satellite TV. The electricity suddenly goes off. She yells out something like "Momma, the electricity is out! Momma, put the generator on! Momma, my video! N'Sync!"*]

IRAQI GIRL:
I hate my momma!
Baba, my father, he said I am smart
but Momma says I am stupid.

I have not been to school
since America came
"You are stupid," she say, "you don't need to go to school."
But I think she didn't like the soldiers cames to our school
they looked like N-Sync, mostly Justin Timberlake,
and they made all the girls to laughing really hard
and since that day she won't let me go to school
because I waved to them.

So I never leave the house.
Even though I can speaks English better than anyone.
My grandparents were scared because they don't speaks English
and soldiers came knocking on their door speaking English
it was the night
but they didn't understand
so they ran to hide under their beds
and a tank, I think it was an Abrams,
they ran the Abrahams into the house
and it took down half the house.
They were eighty years old my grandparents
but they didn't speaks English.

So even we are afraid to sleeps on the roof.
In the summer I used to
put my bed on the roof under the stars
and *Baba,* my father, he used to told me
all the stories of the stars began from Babylon—
it's just down the road past Saddam City—
no,
Sadr City.

We have so much problems on TVs.
On TVs I see suicide bombings

not just for Baghdad but all over Iraq and I felt bad—
but my cousin Karem he says, "No
these are not Iraqis
Iraqis don't know how to kill themselves."

I think something must be secrets because
now we can't go anywheres without
my uncle, Ammu Abdul,
he comes here with his sons, mostly Karem and Khalid,
because we have no men.
But even they haven't taken me to the swimming pool
for two summers now.
Maybe it's dry up?
My friend Lulu, she thinks the Americans are using it.

We don't go anywhere—
really!!!
Momma she doesn't even go to work anymore
she was "let off."
She doesn't leave the house
except to go to the market
with my uncle
and before she goes she covers her hair
she is afraid of getting stolen by gangs—
now they steal women for money
or to sell them.
I try to tell Momma she won't get stolen
her hair is not that nice—
they only steal people whose families have money.
But she says,
"Don't tempt your fates,
now they steal little girls to take them out of the country!"
Today I thought

maybe I should get stolens
so I could leave my country.

On TVs, on *Oprah*, I saw people
they have so many hard lives, at first we feel bad for them
but always by some miracles their things get better!
Today even they showed
Papa Saddam on TVs
and they look through his hair to make fun of him—
"Do you have lice in your hair?" That is always how we tease
in the school when we want to be the most cruel
to the poorest kids.
Do you have lice?
I don't know if he had lice—
but to see it like that he looked like an old man
like a baby.
I felt sorry for him
but I didn't cry.
Momma she cried
she said, "Saddam stole my sons,
he stole my sons"—
I had three brothers who were bigger
I didn't really know them, they were martyrs,
she always says, "Saddam stole my sons"—
so maybe she cries to see him on TVs
thinking, Now he won't give their bones back?
Because she says
"What now?"
"What now?"
"What now?"
She is very—

I am not stupid
I count bombs even
I count between the
hissing when it is high
until the sound becomes low
then two seconds—and it explodes!
If I hear the hissing I know it's in our neighborhood
like in a few blocks
then I hear glass breaking for four seconds
after the hit.
I can tell if it is RPGs or American,
tank or armor vehicle,
Kalashnikov or M16
and I have bullets from both—
but I gave one to Karem, he made a key chain from the M16 bullet
because they are longer and he says "more elegant."
We don't have a machine gun anymore.
Everybody on our street has maybe a pistol or machine gun
in case for troubles.
Now we have a pistol. But only one.
Momma taught me how to use it.

I know I am not stupid—
I found my father's notebooks upstairs
hiding under the floor
he had some math books there and some notebooks—I took this one.
I look to it to keep my head busy
even though the maths are for people bigger than me.
And I can understand some of the maths.
But today
I read in his notebook
that "Sammura,"
that is me—it's dated 5 October, 2002,

"Sammura my beloved was at school
and they asked her
'Have you ever visited Babylon?'
And Sammura, she told them, 'Of course I've been,
even at night because
my father says Saddam put his name on the bricks of Babylon
but he cannot put his name on the stars over Iraq.'
They will arrest me now for this and I am sure to die.
I should have taught her how to lie."

—

I remember some mens came to our house
to take my father—they said
my *baba* is so smart about the stars over Babylon
our president, he needs him.
I have not seen him since I was seven.
Momma thought after the war with America
he might come home
but nobody seen him
and we haven't moved.
I still want to study because if he does comes home
I have to be smarter than when he left.

Actually
I cried today too
when I saw Papa Saddam on TVs
because he stole my father so
I thought he was bigger than anyone
but he didn't even fight to death.
I felt ashames, because why I am afraid from him all my life?
Momma she is right
I am stupid.

[UMM GHADA *lets the* abaya *fall; it is a black hole. A woman of great stillness and pride, peaceful and dispassionate.*]

UMM GHADA:
I named my daughter Ghada.
Ghada means tomorrow.
So I am Umm Ghada, Mother of Ghada.
It is a sign of joy and respect to call a parent by their *kunya*.

In Baghdad, I am famous now as Umm Ghada
because I do live here in yellow trailer
outside Amiriyya bomb shelter
since the bombing
13 February 1991.

Yes I was inside
with nine from my family
talking, laughing
then such a pounding, shaking
everything is fire
I couldn't find my children
I couldn't find my way out
but somehow I did.

In the whole day later
I am searching, searching charred bodies
bodies they were fused together
the only body I did recognize
is my daughter Ghada
so I did take her name [*With so much pride.*]
I am Umm Ghada, Mother of Ghada.

I am hard to understand
why I survive
and my children dead.
I asked to Allah why?
Why you make me alive?
That night all people died
four hundred three people
and there's nothing we can do. They are dead.

This trailer is my witness stand.
All photos on this wall—and here—are me
with emissaries from the world
who come to Amiriyya shelter to look
what really happen here
not what they read in papers
or see in the CNN.
Here is guest book they all sign,
your name will be witness too.
La, I must show it to you first. *Ta`al.*

[*She enters the shelter; it is the first time we see her subtle limp.*]

This is Amiriyya bomb shelter.
Here they write names
in chalk over the smoked figures.
Here, on the ceiling, you can see
charred handprints and footprints
from people who lay in the top bunks.
And here a silhouette of a woman
vaporized from heat.
This huge room became an oven,
and they pressed to the walls to escape from the flames.

In the basement too
bombs burst the pipes
hot water came up to five feet
and boiled the people.

La, la, I do not want to show you there
it is too much
the walls are stuck with hairs and skin.

Come, I will take you to the roof
you can see how the hole was made.

[*As she walks toward the hole in the roof, we hear the midday call to
prayer off in the distance; she pauses briefly.*]

Two bombs from U.S. airplane
come to this point of the roof.
The first bomb is drilling bomb
drilled this hole
second one
come inside exactly same spot
and exploded in fires.

The U.S. said they thought this is
communication center for military.
Myself,
I think they were testing bomb—
these bomb had never been use before, but it is special
two-bomb design for breaking only a bomb shelter.
It is very purpose.
It is very purpose.

Now look around this hole
wild greens they are growing
life did choose to root
here in this grave of Iraqi people.

All my family is here, Ghada is here
so I am Umm Ghada, Mother of Tomorrow.
My full name is dead with them.

Come.
Now you sign the witness book.

[LAYAL *picks up a paintbrush.*]

LAYAL:
What now?
What now?
What now?

We have a story—
There is a restaurant with a sign
COME IN, EAT ALL YOU WANT,
FREE OF CHARGE
YOUR GRANDSON WILL PAY THE BILL.
So a young man, a teenager,
he goes in
happy for the free meal,
he eats, and eats, and eats
when he is done eating all he wants
the waiter brings him a bill.
The young man says to the waiter,
"No, your sign says free of charge,
my grandson will pay the bill."

The waiter says, "Yes, indeed sir,
but this—
this is your grandfather's bill." [*She laughs.*]

My grandfather's bill!

You know my house was hit, from Bush's war, *aa, aa*—
I wasn't there, *il-hamdu lillah,*
but we lost everything, my paintings for the new exhibition
my family's things, everything.
That's why I'm living here, at my sister's house
it was only eight houses from here—
this neighborhood they bomb, Mansur, can you believe it?
So how smart is this bomb
if it bomb a painter? [*She laughs.*]
Maybe they think I am dangerous?

Maybe I am, I am attached like I will die if I leave.

I think you're dangerous—
most Americans they are not so attached this way
they feel so free, even to be alone
they are not tied to each other or to anyone.
I am afraid to be alone
I don't want freedom—to be alone?
I don't care for it, I like protection
all I want is to feel it, love—

I am crazy for it,
I am hungry every morning like I have never eaten before,
and there is never enough to feed me
so when I find more
I risk everything for it

oblivion even, I don't care
I submit completely.
And still I am empty
I never feel worth
because I shouldn't be so hungry
because others are not so hungry
or they can control it—but I cannot control myself
I cannot keep my mind from flesh.

I tell you, even when I fell in love
not with my husband
after I was married
really I fell in love
it humiliated me
to finally see
how much of myself I could never be
and I hated it
not to be full
not to feel whole
it's the worst feeling this occupation
to inhabit your body but not to be able to live in it.

So I had an affair! [*She laughs.*]
I let myself love him—
we were just a boy and a girl in art school
painting, drawing, expressive
you can't imagine the freedoms
we had teachers from all over the world coming to Baghdad
I was very messy
and when my husband found out
he shot me.

I thought I was dead.

And even in the emergency room I was saying,
"No it was me
with the gun, it was me, it was an accident."
We never spoke about it
but he never stopped me from having an affair again!

I think
most women they must be so hungry
because they love with such a sacrifice
an aching
but I tell you,
when you're this way
so attached
always loving like you will die without something—
you love like an Iraqi woman! [*Laughing.*] Shahrazad!
Oh Americans they have this passion to save everything
because they have such a big footprint, they feel guilty.
They are a very handsome teenager
so tall and strong and
passionate, selfish, charming
but they don't think.

You have
our war now
inside you, like a burden, like an orphan
with freedom, intelligence, all opportunity and choice
yet we tether you to something so old you cannot see it—
we have you chained
to the desert
to your blood
you carry it in you—its lifetimes
and you fight your war to unchain yourself
you come back

you feel at home here
maybe different
maybe more than in your country—
but you hate us too
because you cannot breathe
because women here are not free—
and you are not free, you love too much.
It's the same, all, anywhere you live
if you love like an Iraqi woman
if you love like you cannot breathe.

[*Huddled,* THE AMERICAN *hasn't left her studio apartment in New York City for days; she is glued to the TV.*]

THE AMERICAN:
Now they're digging through mass graves with their bare hands
and one guy on TV I saw him
he found a pack of cigarettes
and he said my brother smoked
this kind of cigarette
so this is my brother's body
and he took the bones with him
so he could bury them
what he thought
was his brother.

I've never seen men cry like that.

I watch my dad
try not to cry
because when he's watching TV
and it's green
nighttime footage of

bombs
he can recognize the street
and the neighborhoods
where all his family
lives
still.

I watch TV
looking for
faces
of our family
so all I do is cry.
But my dad he can't
so
he ends up choking and
making himself
sick
I mean
he's lived here in the U.S.
for forty years
he plays golf
five times a week.
He's just sad
but contained
because you
can't
you just can't
watch it
on TV.
I'm on my knees
in the middle of my apartment
with my mom
on the phone

watching
I'm holding a rosary
watching
CNN
I want to pray
but I don't have
words
so I say their names
out loud
Sati`,
Zuhayr,
Huda,
Zuhira,
Behnam,
Rabab,
over and over trying
to see them
alive
because we don't know
anything
we can't
call
we can't get through on the phones
still
and
now
now people are burying their dead in their backyard
in their garden
the football field
it's every day
a police station
my uncle Sati` lives next to a police station
my uncle Zuhayr lives next to the airport

Amma Huda—next to the Palestine Hotel
Amma Zuhira—in Karrada—Mount Lebanon
my cousin Maysoon she used to work for the UN
but the whole face got blown off—I'm reading on the bus—

They never forget ever.
They carry everything with them.
I mean everything they are, they're so attached like
great-grandparents, parents, children
it lives in them, walks with them
they can't let go
of anything
they hold it all inside them.
So when they cry
it's lifetimes
I've never seen anything like it.

HUDA:
I can't move
I am here in London now
this is where my husband died, in this house
and I didn't change a thing from that time I kept the house the same,
his picture, everything.
I was invited to go back,
so many people I was working with have returned but
I have moved five times in my life—always fleeing
Baghdad, Lebanon, Istanbul, Baghdad again, anyway.
America offered me lots of money to go back
but I don't believe in this, some Iraqis
they are just selling themselves.

I said let the young ones living there have a chance with the policies
but they are too afraid to speak up

they are shell-shocked, all these girls
they go backward
they abandon their education and now,
now they are wearing the veils.
Their grandmothers are more liberated than them.

I am in a period of disheartenment everywhere.
Maybe I should be there.
I don't know what to do with myself now, I have doubts, yeah, well
about my whole life.
I don't feel I have achieved what I wanted, my potential.
The worst thing I fear most now is civil war.
Iraqis don't want to be cut up, to be separated.
Ya`ni, we had fine interrelations
my family married with the Shi`a, my husband was a Kurd
there was no segregation sort of thing—these people
they have been living together in this area for thousands of years.
If we want to sculpt a nation
we cannot hack away at it
without a plan for the human being.
Each moment is vital—

I wanted, we all wanted Saddam to go during the Gulf War
that was our moment—the people made this big rebellion—
sixteen of the eighteen provinces fell
and they were sure America would help them
but America turned its back. America made a no-fly zone
but when they saw Saddam going with his helicopters
to execute his own people
they allowed him to fly. It was a bloodbath,
Saddam killed tens of thousands, trucks full,
and buried them just mass graves.
Then the worst thirteen years' suffering—

This what do you call it? *Hisar?* Embargo?
And it made Saddam stronger
and the country more backward and religious,
and funny enough Saddam he was never religious,
but when the middle class
were selling their books on the street in order to eat
they felt the whole world had abandoned them.
And this isolation mentality cannot now be changed suddenly—
this thirteen years' embargo
just gave the fundamentalists their legitimacy.

I mean look how they are voting. I don't recognize my country.

The mistake is not the war, no, America had to do it
the mistake was supporting Saddam all his life.
All the Arab countries too—they treated him like a buddy, a king
giving him all these weapons to fight this eight years' war with Iran,
and he gassed Halabja, he drained the marshes—
And finally, after all these years, finally they found him
an old man in a hole
and they want to give this man a fair trial?
No.
He was always who he is—he is a savage.

It's a cycle, repeating. Fallujah, Najaf,
the golden mosque—Samarra—

We are fighting for who they will trust—

I don't believe anymore in revolution, *ya`ni*,
the concept of revolution to change the values
development must grow carefully, gradually, not suddenly
it has to grow more deep rooted.

Even though I can say
we all can say
congratulations
the regime is gone.
Saddam is gone.

[NANNA *is an old woman, scrappy and shrewd; she has seen it all. She is selling anything she can on the street corner. She wears the* abaya *traditionally over her head so only her face and hands remain showing. The third call to prayer sounds in the distance.*]

NANNA:
Hallo hallo
you like to buy?
These things very nice
very old
from good family.
We have old
no
not that old.
Not ancient.

Hallo hallo
I'm here, here
always here
this my spot.
I see things
I see everything—

I saw the looting
these are not Iraqis
Iraqis are not so degraded as this—
but maybe

some people
took
bricks
from
palaces
only.
There were too many anyway.

I heard a marines saying
"Go in Ali Baba—go in
 take what is yours."
Aa, they wanted us to have
everything!
It's freedom to have!
Chal chal alayya!

I have too much existence
I have lived through twenty-three revolutions
my life has been spared—
if my life has been spared
to whom do I owe my debt?
I have so much to repay.
To whom do I owe my debt?

[*She spots another customer.*]

Hallo hallo you like to buy?
We have very old,
very special old—

OK, OK,

[*She chooses to confide in her original customer but only at a whisper.*]

I saw
Iraqi peoples
bringing petrol,
shhh
and
burning
all
National Archives,
Qur'anic Library,
all—
it was not accident
I saw a map
they knew what to take
they were told what to take
and nobody stopped them
and they
burned them gone.
Our history is finished.
Sunni, Shi`a, Kurd,
Christian even, Jew—
if they take what we share,
it is easier
to finish.

It's revenge
no
God's revenge
upon us
because we didn't—
we were tested and
we didn't
finish
get rid of

Saddam
ourselves
we
deserve
maybe
we were
silent
our history is—

When I was young in the school
they had us to draw
our family tree—
my mother had a new dress
it's with ruffle and flowers
that I loved
and she wear it in the house
I think every day for many weeks.
So I draw my mother like a big flower
with ruffles.
My teacher say no
it is wrong before Allah
drawing her hair and her body showing—
I am disrespecting.
So I look to the other children and
they drawing only the fathers and grandfathers
because of the name line.

So I just erased her, my mother
it was only pencil.

THE AMERICAN:
Here
there's space

we throw our arms wide
amber alerts and
seven men get trapped underground
and we stop everything
we fly in engineers
to save
everything
we make a movie
we go on *Oprah,* we talk about it
like we are moving on
or maybe
we can't move on
but just one trauma we say
OK
this can change you
possibly
your psychology, for the rest of your life
OK.
But there's no one saying—

when their parents get
blown apart
in front of their eyes
or their sons
are kidnapped
trying to go to work
or hacked
to death
or there's a tank in my *ammu*'s front yard—
or they survive
everything
over and over and over again for as many years as I've been alive
my cousins

who are, who could have been
the same as me
told me they wouldn't
get married
because if they
someday
saw a chance to get out
they had to take it
and not look back.
They never stop looking back.
The three that escaped
they had to watch it on TV
the second war
they said maybe it's worse seeing it on TV
sick, they can't protect the family.
But my dad said
maybe it's better
for the
future
but if we lose
just one
one
it won't be
worth it.

Behnam
Rabab
Ammar
Bashshar
Nassar
Luma

—

I should get out
get something to
eat.
I'm fat.
I should just go to the gym and run.
God I'm so stressed out
maybe
I should take a yoga class instead?

Anyway I can watch it at the gym
people work out
to the war
on three channels.
They drink beer at the bar to the war.
I mean, I'm blond
I hear everything people say.
I can't stop
I wake up and fall asleep with the TV on
holding a rosary
watching—
I know
I should just
turn it off
but I can't
I hate it when people say
I don't watch
it
anymore
it depresses me
yeah
it depresses me
I can't
breathe—

I'm sick
my stomach
I can't get out of my—
it's a beautiful warm day
and I'm a cave.
I can't walk down the street
and see people smiling—
dragging bodies through the street
for the rest of my life
Iraqis are animals cheering, dragging bodies through the street.
But my family can't even leave their house
and I can't call
still
and we're
smiling
pointing
at
a man
naked
with a sandbag on his head
raped
with a chemical light, told to masturbate.
I cannot carry it
and they're
thumbs-up
smiling
don't tell me
they didn't know
their job
not with smiling
every photo
they were
smiling.

How can I ever
go home again
and sit
in my *amma*'s kitchen
and say
I'm sorry
I'm sorry
I'm—
we just keep going
subway
rush rush
Christmas shopping
and
the war, it's all so heartbreaking don't you think?
I don't even know
hundreds of thousands?
How many Iraqis?
And
a woman actually turned to me
and said that
she said
"The war it's all so heartbreaking"
she was getting a pedicure.
I was getting a fucking pedicure.
I walk
I can't walk
down
the street
I want
New York to stop.
Why don't we count the number of Iraqi dead?

Why?

LAYAL:
Why are you here?

Don't look at me like that
always this pressure on me
I can't bear it—your look.

You tell me about freedom, about choice and possibilities,
and then you look at me like a whore for choosing
to paint myself naked
and you look at me like a whore for choosing
to paint portraits of Saddam
and now you look at me like a whore for thinking, just thinking,
to do this mosaic for the floor of the Rashid Hotel?
But what are you creating with your freedom?
I am more free than you.

You beg me to leave
to get out while I can, I am getting too involved
insisting I get out for my safety.

Why? What is safe? There is no safe.

I wish I were afraid
I am beyond afraid—
I am just running, running
straight into it
always like this I am running
since the day my husband shot me
because I should have been dead
but I wasn't—
So what am I?
Why am I alive?

To be made love to—passed around from one man to another
his cousin, his brother, the ministers of—
and now—

I am aware that I will die.
I am complicit. Where else can I go with my hate?
Who will protect me but the regime?
Always I run to them, I come crying, begging, take care of me
they need me to do it, oh they love me to run to them crying—
If I am not afraid then there is no feeling.

Your eyes say to me that I am a whore
their eyes say I am the most beautiful woman in Baghdad
I am their fountain
I have been raped and raped and raped and raped
and I want more
they see me, they recognize me for what I am
that is freedom
they will never kill me—

HUDA:
—we just woke up
we heard a shot and gunfire and things and
we thought it would pass and something would happen
nothing—
we gathered all the friends, in the street you know
to see what's going to happen,
and we never went back to our house—
this was the coup, 1963—it was a Friday.
They came with their Kalashnikovs and their boots and so on
going house by house arresting people.
I was held, eh, two-and-a-half months,
my husband four-and-a-half months,

we were pro–Abd al-Karim Qasim, we were the leftists.
One hundred eighty thousand people
were just arrested from Baghdad and all the elite
you know, the artists and architects—everybody, intellectuals—
we were Communist then but not violent, the Ba`thist only took us
because we disagreed.

The prison status was terrible
we stayed lying on the floor
only lying like sardines. We were naked.
I remember one woman she got her period.
You know what they do when a woman gets her period?
They hang her upside down naked
so her blood runs on her, for her whole cycle like that, upside down.
Anyway. That was that.

The fearsome thing was that every night at sort of two o'clock
we heard the gates and chains opening
and they'd call a list of women and they'd take them and
they wouldn't come back.
We could hear things, all night, always rape,
or rape with electronic instruments.
But their way, I promise you, their way
was to torture the people close to you
that is how they'd do it.
One woman I was with
they brought her baby, three-months-old baby, outside the cell
they put this woman's baby in a bag with starving cats
they tape-recorded the sound of this and of her rape
and they played it
for her husband in his cell.
That is how they do it.

So how these people could have liberated themselves?

Anyway, nightmare.

When we got out of jail we made passports, fake passports,
and we fled across the desert with our wet clothes on our back.
I did washing
but we didn't wait to dry them. [*She laughs and hacks.*]

Myself, too, it takes a lifetime to be liberated.

OK, are you hungry? I'm having another whiskey.

[*She pours herself another drink.*]

You think the people don't want liberation?
For every one Iraqi police officer who dies
there are two hundred more
desperate to risk everything
waiting in line with their applications
to take his place.
How many Iraqi police have died?
Protect them, empower them.
Otherwise to live like this it is not liberation it is masochism.

[*A loud bombing raid; everything is shaking.* LAYAL *is screaming into
the phone.*]

LAYAL:
When is this going to stop?

I don't care what time it is
Why don't you do something about it?

I hear the sounds—something—like it's in my house
and I can't make it through another one.

La, targets!
How they blow up a house in this neighborhood?
This is rich neighborhood
and they say it is an accident?
No, it is on purpose or stupidity!
How they do it?
Why my house?
I feel like an animal every time I hear that sound.
I am tired, I want my house back—

No I am sorry—

no, eh—
of course it's late, your wife, she's next to you
I'm just, I am angry and I don't know where to be in this.

No, my husband he sleeps upstairs
he can sleep through anything.

Don't ask me now again.
I told you I don't know how to do mosaic—
I am a painter, why he wants me?
I don't know how.

La, don't tell him I don't want to do it—just tell him
I am not so good at it
I have no knowledge for mosaic.
OK, I think about it
I'm just angry now and
why can't you do something?

Oh
not tonight I mean—

No of course, I think of you
I'm
I'll come tomorrow
OK
at your office
OK.
Fine. Fine. Fine.

[LAYAL *hangs up the phone.*]

Shahryar!

I said yes to the mosaic.

[*A voice-over cuts in. It is a man's voice on a telephone answering machine. His voice is loud and urgent. It is* THE AMERICAN'S *uncle calling her from Baghdad.*]

UNCLE [*first phone call*]:
Hallo hallo hallo
I am your uncle calling from Baghdad.
We have tried to phone you since Tuesday.
We are very sorry—

THE AMERICAN:
—it's just his beautiful broken English
he calls me his heart's
daughter
my uncle Behnam
trying

to reach me
for three days
they saw the dust and the papers blowing
everything they saw New York on TV.
He called to say
he was sorry
can you believe that?
Sorry for my great city
hopes this never happens again—
all the family
worried sick about me.
And
my mom's family in Michigan
they all called my parents in Michigan to see if I was OK
I know they love me but
they didn't call me personally
and my Iraqi family are calling from halfway around the world
calling New York
they didn't stop until
they heard my voice.

Our last conversation
was before the bombs started in Baghdad
I finally got through to my aunt
and I'm screaming into the phone
"I'm calling from New York"—

UNCLE [*second phone call, again on voice-over*]:
Hallo hallo hallo
we have tried to phone you since Tuesday
we are very sorry to hear this terrible things happen.
Our family worry about you—

[LAYAL *rushes to the phone to answer it.*]

LAYAL:
Hallo! Hallo! Sabah? *Habibti!* My daughter!
Shlonich?
Aa, aa, fine, fine we are OK, OK,
how are you?

Aa, aa, I know our phones they don't work for sure. [*She laughs.*]

I'm calling for three week but we couldn't get through
oh *habibti,* my daughter, I kiss you, I hold you oh, I miss you
I miss you, *habibti*
I miss you—

La—don't come home
not this summer.
Stay
take some summer classes or
why not go to your aunt's house in London? *Aa?*

La, la—
It's, getting sort of
well it's getting very hot already and, eh
the air-condition is broken
we are old-fashioned now even me, who can believe it?

Sabah, it is too hot for you to come home!

[*The line is cut off.*]

Sabah? Hallo?
Hallo?

Sabah?
Sabah?

[*Devastated,* LAYAL *drops the phone.*]

UNCLE [*third phone call, again on voice-over*]:
Hallo hallo
we are very sorry to hear this terrible things happen.
Our family worry about you.
We hope you are always well
and wish you all the happiness.
Again we are deeply deeply sorry
and hope this will never happen again.
We love you very much.
All the family does love you.
We are waiting for you to visit us.
You must come and visit us.
It is very hard for us to come to you
but you must come here
and visit us.
And you must bring your father
and you must bring your mother
and you must bring your brother.
We are waiting for you—
we miss you very much, all the family,
your uncles and aunts with their children
and we love you—
we are waiting for you.

THE AMERICAN:
"I'm calling from New York," I'm screaming into the phone,
our last call before the bombs started and
my *amma* Ramza finally picks up the phone

the first thing she says to me
clear as English is
"Go to church and pray"
her only other English is I love you
I love you
habibti, habibti
I love you
I love you
I love you
I love you
I love you
I love you
I love you
I love you
I love you
Behnam
Rabab
Ammar
Bashshar
Nassar
Luma
Fadhila
Mazin
Zena
Nadia
Zuhayr
Mufida
Karem
Rashid
Muther
Zuhira
Jaber
Geanne

Siba
Reem
Rand
Ramza
Zaki
Aubai
Rawah
Raid
Mary
Jacob
Muna
Huda
Nabil
Myriam
Salma
Adnan
Fadiya
Layth
Maysoon
Yousif
Zayd
Sa`ad
Salaam
Basil
Sati`
Aamira
Milad
Masarra
I love you
I love you
I love you
I love you
I love you

I love you
I love you
I love you
I love you
I love you
I love you
I love you
I love you
I love you
I love you
I love you
I love you
I love you
I love you
I love you
I love you, I love you
on and on like that
five minutes, ten minutes
until they cut the phones off.

And—

LAYAL:
I will never leave
not for freedom you do not even have
call me what you like, look at me how you will
I tell you
so many women have done the same as me
everywhere they have to do the same.
If I did the same in your England or America
wouldn't they call me a whore there too?
Your Western culture, sister, will not free me
from being called a whore

not my sex
women are not free
go home
you are cold, you are a cave
go back to your safety.

I will do whatever he asks of me.
But this
I do this for me, this is for me—

[*Suddenly genuinely amused.*]

I will make the mosaic of Bush's face
on the floor of the Rashid Hotel
and I will write in English for all the world to read
BUSH IS CRIMINAL.
Why not? What's the worst?
Everyone walking into the hotel
will walk across his face.
And I will walk across his face.

[LAYAL *begins to destroy her art studio. She smashes pottery and anything she can find as she looks to make the pieces for the mosaic.*]

And two hundred more
waiting in line
risking everything to take my place
without my legs
buried in the backyard
they're making their own map of
me anyway—sure after every
bomb
first bomb drilling bomb

all I want is to feel it—love
we were just a boy and a girl
bodies were fused together—
second bomb come inside exactly same spot
here—he made them prostitutes
eight houses from here
don't come home
I am not the Layal he loved
third bomb—boil the people
I don't want freedom
Mullaya why are you here?
so old you cannot see it
yaboo yaboo
I'm fine I'm fine I'm [LAYAL *begins to beat her face and chest.*]
la ilaha illa allah [*The fourth call to prayer is heard.*]
la ilaha illa allah
la ilaha illa allah

I'm dead.

[*The* MULLAYA *continues* LAYAL's *pace and fractured language with-out pause. However, what was for* LAYAL *explosive and destructive is for the* MULLAYA *effortless.*]

MULLAYA:
A silhouette of a woman
vaporized from heat
in a void
deserted
fighting to keep transparency
my body but her body
herself inside me
why do you look at us as we have two hearts?

we have only one heart
you know us better
and all what is left of us
Baba oh *Baba*
I have too much existence
I have lived through seven thousand revolutions

to the well one day you'll return
thirsty, assured it will be there
but you'll not find—spring, nor river
so beware of throwing a stone
into the well
paint with real restraint
always fight to keep transparency
because once you go past
between the shore and the river
it goes muddy, it's muddy forever
the marshes are witness
if you drink water out of the well
it's the space you leave empty from the beginning

look
around this whole
I'm afraid to see them
when they're grown
wild greens they are growing
life did choose to root
here in this grave
all my family is here
same accent
same eyes
same nature
very big heart

we couldn't live together like this?
always it is life and death
and life and death—

[*She steps into the river, raising water to her face. As she continues
she becomes fully immersed.*]

carry it with you
so when they cry
so old you cannot see it
try to reach me
for three days
hear my voice
upside-down
broken English
collecting
carrying
house by house
I can't move
I can't breathe
I cannot choose to leave
throw our arms wide
sing to my mother
I am home again
oblivion even
I don't care
I submit completely

late in the evening
I come to collect worn souls from the river
because
I love you
I love you

I love you
I love you
I fear it here
and I love it here
I cannot stop what I am here
either I shall die
or I shall live a ransom for all the daughters
of savagery.
She called it Savagery
when you love like you cannot breathe.

[*We hear the fifth and final call to prayer. Darkness, it is the end of the day's cycle.* NANNA *continues to gather the few props, which are indeed everything she now owns, to sell on the street corner.*]

NANNA:
Hallo hallo
hallo hallo
you like to buy?
These things very nice, very old,
from good family
we have books
carpet
shoes.

Hallo hallo
you like this painting?

[NANNA *reaches for* LAYAL's *painting.*]

It is very worth
she call it *Savagery*
famous artist

her name
Layal—

You recognize? *Aa,*
I was her neighbor
I knew her good
bomb fell her house
la, la, again, another bomb, her sister house,
she dead
her husband dead
her daughter blind.
Aa, aa, very sad—
so it is more worth
more worth!

She is martyr, all of us
all, the president he used to love her, he praise her
he put her painting in
Baghdad museum of arts.
It was full only his portrait
room and room of him
and I did saw it
he put her body, her trees
next to his face.
You must buy, buy
you must buy.

I tell you
this her last painting alive
all the rest
they are burned dead in the museum
I run
I took it.

Our history is finish
so it is more worth
more worth.

I give you secret
some trees are womans
this one, little one, is me
I let her paint me
aa, she see me
shhh
don't say
my husband he thinks it's just a tree.

I have to sell it
I have to eat
two dollar?

[NANNA's *hand is outstretched and open.*]

two dollar?

PRODUCTION NOTES

Heather Raffo's 9 Parts of Desire was conceived as a one-woman show. Although the solo actress plays nine separate characters, through her the audience sees what could also be conflicting aspects of a single psyche. As the play begins, individual characters are introduced slowly, and the movement from role to role is careful and distinct. But the pace quickens, time frames blur, and characters cut each other off midsentence, driving the play toward a psychic civil war with the solo performer embodying the larger argument of what liberation means for each woman and for Iraq.

Similarly, the artist Layal embraces this larger struggle for self-identity and liberation. Layal begins the play embodying the stories of many Iraqi women as she works. Layal says:

> I paint my body
> but her body, herself inside me.
> So it is not me alone
> it is all of us
> but I am the body that takes the experience.

However, at the end of the play, when Layal is closest to death, she willfully explodes under the weight of the many women she has taken on. Her psyche fractures, and she speaks using fragments of lines we have heard throughout the play in the other characters' language. When Layal dies, the Mullaya, a professional mourner in her ancient role, carefully picks up these broken pieces of language and builds a greater and celebratory whole from them. I see the end of the play as the Mullaya's build to the final:

She called it Savagery
when you love like you cannot breathe.

With this the work is named. Nanna's selling of the painting *Savagery* functions then as an epilogue to remind us finally that everything we have witnessed has a price.

If the play is produced with a multiactor cast, I still encourage the doubling of roles—to cast, for instance, three women rather than nine. When we see an actress transform from one Iraqi woman to another, we are better reminded of the complexities of nationality and the universality of all women. Layal, Huda, and the American have always been at the core of the play's dialogue, with the other characters playing supporting roles. I therefore encourage separate casting for Layal, Huda, and the American, with the remaining voices divided at the director's discretion.

In development with director Joanna Settle for its New York premiere, the play grew to include the prologue by the Mullaya and focused less on Layal and her art studio as the play's home. The stage came to represent various levels of Iraqi society from the ancient to the modern: crumbling tiles; layers of mosaic; bricks, books, carpets, and sandbags. At the center of the production was a river, a reminder of Iraq's heritage as the cradle of civilization. The river was both mythic and functional, a symbol of a life-giving source and of the underworld. Layal's paintbrushes came out of the river; Huda's books and newspapers lined the river; they became Nanna's looted books and newspapers. Every single item onstage was part of every character's life. Nothing was left without multiple purposes. If building a river is not an option, the use of water somewhere, whether it be from a bowl or another vessel, would still allude to this imagery and symbolize its central function connecting all of the women.

Similarly, the *abaya* works as a unifying prop rather than a costume piece. The actress's use of the *abaya* to transform from character to character is key. It broadens and challenges the audience's understanding of the image. The *abaya* is a traditional robelike garment that has long been worn by both women and men in Iraq. It is not a veil, and it never covers the face. The *abaya*'s origin is functional, and it offers possible freedoms and/or oppressions to those who wear it. In the West, it has now become a symbol of all Iraqi women. However, many women in Iraq have never worn it. I would therefore like to encourage a real freedom in the exploration of the many theatrical and unconventional uses for this simple piece of black fabric.

This show rejects stereotypes on many levels. Iraq is a great melting pot, and its women vary from fair and blond to dark skinned and black haired. Historically, Iraq has been one of the most secular countries in the Middle East, and its women some of the most educated. It would be wrong to overdramatize for the sake of a political point or to use the women for sympathy by focusing on the injustice, the anger, or the intensely emotional. I would encourage those doing a production of *9 Parts of Desire* never to think of these women as victims or portray them sentimentally but rather to explore the resilience, ambitions, warmth, humor, integrity, and ancient history of the Iraqi women depicted here.

GLOSSARY OF ARABIC TERMS AND SONGS

AA

Yes.

ABAYA

A garment worn in some areas of the Persian Gulf region. In Iraq, it is usually a square, long-sleeved, floor-length, loose, black garment worn over other clothing. It is worn by both men and women. Men wear it hanging from their shoulders; women wear it hanging off the top of their heads.

ABD AL-KARIM QASIM

An Iraqi military officer born in Baghdad, Qasim (1914–63) organized the 1958 military coup that overthrew the pro-British monarchy. He became prime minister of the new republic. In contrast to the monarchy he was seen as a nationalist leader. He was responsible for the 1958 interim constitution establishing equality regardless of religion, race, or nationality. His reign was marked by increased access to education and resources, land reform, and other progressive measures. Qasim was against Iraq joining the greater United Arab Republic and in turn kept down the pan-Arab Ba`th Party. On February 9, 1963, he was overthrown and executed when the Ba`th party staged its first military coup and took control of Iraq. Earlier, Qasim had escaped an assassination attempt on his life led by Saddam Hussein, who afterward fled to Egypt.

AMAL

A woman's name meaning "hope."

AMMA

Aunt.

AMMU

Uncle.

APSU AND TIAMAT

In the epic of creation *Enuma Elish* (ca. 2000 B.C.), Apsu and Tiamat are the water god and goddess who become the father and mother of all creation.

BABA

Father.

BABYLON

The ancient capital of Babylonia, in Mesopotamia (in contemporary Iraq, about 55 miles south of Baghdad). The name is the Greek form of "Babel," which is derived in turn from the Semitic form *bab-ilû*, "God's Gate." This in turn is a translation of the Sumerian *Kadmirra*. The city was probably the largest in the world from about 1770 to 1670 B.C. and once again from about 612 to 320 B.C. and was the site of the Hanging Gardens, one of the Seven Wonders of the World.

BA`THIST

A member of the Ba`th party. The Ba`th party is a secular pan-Arab party. It was founded in Syria in 1945 and came to power in Iraq in 1963. Saddam Hussein took total control of the Ba`th party in Iraq in 1979 when he assumed the presidency. Beginning with and throughout the Iraq-Iran War (1980–88) the party grew to have a strong focus on the military. Under Saddam it became nearly impossible to hold any position and advance in the public sector without becoming a member of the Ba`th party and few citizens could avoid joining, at least nominally. After the 1991 Gulf War and throughout the sanctions imposed on Iraq (1990–2003), both the state and the party were weakened, forcing the regime to depend more on tribal loyalties and to distance itself from secularism.

BEDOUIN

A generic name for a desert dweller, the term describes a member of a nomadic group inhabiting the desert region in the Middle East.

CALIPH

An old term for the leader of the Islamic community. It comes from the Arabic word *khalifah,* which means "successor," meaning a successor to the prophet Muhammad.

CHAL CHAL

A verb in the Iraqi dialect (*kalkala* in classical Arabic) meaning to "engulf." A traditional Baghdadi song modernized by the popular singer Ilham al-Madfa`I starts with the well-known lines *chal chal alayya 'l-rumman, Numi fiza`li* (The pomegranate [branches] have engulfed me and lemons have come to the rescue. I do not desire this beauty, just take me home!). While the song appears to be a love song on the surface, it is also interpreted allegorically as a reference to Iraq around the time of World War I being a battleground between the waning Ottoman Empire (pomegranate) which had ruled it for centuries and the British (lemons) who occupied it in 1917 under the guise of liberation.

CHE MALI WALI

The title of a traditional Iraqi song, "Because I Have No Ruler [Protector]." The lyrics are as follows:

che mali wali	Because I have no protector
buya smallah	by God, [oh dear!]
mit'adhiba bi dinyay	I am tortured in my life
ya baba	oh Daddy, [oh dear!]
che mali wali	because I have no protector.
battah w siditni	Like a duck and you hunted me
buya smallah	by God, [oh dear!]

bein al juruf wil mayy	between the shore and the river.
ya baba	Oh Daddy, [oh dear!]
battah w siditini	like a duck and you hunted me
yal ma riditni	you who did not want me
buya smallah	by God, [oh dear!]
tiksir janahi leish	why break my wings?
ya baba	Oh Daddy, [oh dear!]
yal ma riditni	you who did not want me
kho tidri biyeh	you know me better,
buya smallah	by God, [oh dear!]
mali gulub ithnein	I do not have two hearts,
ya baba, kho tidri biyeh	Oh Daddy, [oh dear!]
	you know me better
wa shdhall iliyeh	and what am I left with?
buya smallah	By God, [oh dear!]
wahid w akhadhteh wiyak	my one heart you took with you.
ya baba, wa shdhall iliyeh	Oh Daddy, [oh dear!]
	and what am I left with?

—Translation by Salaam Yousif

ERIDU, QURNA, UR

Three ancient cities and villages, all located within the current boundaries of
Iraq. Each is thought to be a possible site of the Garden of Eden. Ur was one
of the earliest settlements in southern Mesopotamia and the largest city in
the world in the second and third centuries B.C. It is also believed to be the
birthplace of the monotheistic patriarch Abraham and is mentioned in the
Bible.

GHADA

Tomorrow.

HABIBTI

Darling, sweetheart.

HALABJA

A Kurdish village in northern Iraq that suffered a devastating chemical attack under Saddam Hussein.

HARAM

"Sin" or "forbidden." Also used to mean "what a pity."

HISAR

"Embargo," referring to the years of UN sanctions imposed on Iraq from the end of the Gulf War in 1991 to the U.S.-led invasion in March 2003. Although designed to weaken Saddam's regime, the embargo also deprived ordinary Iraqis of basic necessities resulting in the deaths of thousands of civilians.

HUDA

A woman's name meaning "the way" or "God's way," "enlightenment."

IL-HAMDU LILLAH

"Praise be to God " or "Thank God."

IL-MAWT YIHRIG IL-GLUB

"Death burns the heart"—an Iraqi proverb.

KARRADA

A middle-class neighborhood in central Baghdad with many shops.

KUNYA

An honorific term used to refer to parents in relation to their first-born son.

For instance, if a child is named Omar, the parents would respectfully be referred to as Abu Omar (father of Omar) and Umm Omar (mother of Omar). It is not a common practice to take the name of a daughter, unless the parent has no sons. A *kunya* is often used respectfully instead of a parent's own first name.

KURD

An Indo-Iranian, non-Arab population that inhabits the transnational region known as Kurdistan, a plateau and mountain area in southwest Asia including parts of Iraq, Turkey, and Iran and smaller sections of Syria and Armenia. Comprising more than thirty million people, it is the world's largest ethnic group without its own state. Iraqi Kurdish populations suffered political and social injustices under Saddam, including the infamous Anfal campaign and chemical gassing of the Kurdish city of Halabja where thousands were killed or displaced.

LA

No.

LA ILAHA ILLA ALLAH

An Arabic phrase meaning "there is no God but God." It is the first half of the Muslim profession of faith. It is also uttered upon witnessing or hearing of a sad or calamitous event.

LAYAL

A woman's name meaning "nights."

MANSUR

An upscale neighborhood in Baghdad.

MARSH ARABS

Inhabitants of the marshes in southern Iraq near where the Tigris and Euphrates rivers meet. Direct descendants of the original Mesopotamian cultures (Babylonian and Sumerian), the Marsh Arabs have maintained their way of life for thousands of years. The marshes are a unique ecosystem in the Middle East supporting a wide variety of plant and animal life not commonly found in desert regions. Marsh Arabs live in reed huts built on top of the water; also constructed from reeds are canoes, barges, and large *mudhifs* (guest houses). Their primary trades are fishing, farming, and raising of water buffalo. Marsh Arabs are primarily Shi`a. During the Iran-Iraq war of the 1980s the relatively inhospitable marshlands were a place of refuge for soldiers defecting from the war. The Marsh Arabs also participated in the 1991 uprisings against Saddam Hussein following the Gulf War. As punishment, Saddam built a series of dams to divert the flow of the Tigris and Euphrates rivers away from the marshes. Much of the wetlands regions were turned into desert, and the Marsh Arabs were forced out of their homes. Subsequently, a culture and population primarily untouched for five thousand years was uprooted. Some Marsh Arabs remain, but most are refugees living in other areas of Iraq or have emigrated to Iran.

MOUNT LEBANON (HOTEL)

A hotel in Baghdad in the Karrada district that was the site of a devastating car bomb on March 17, 2004, that destroyed most of the hotel and nearby houses. Victims of the bombing were primarily Iraqis living in the hotel.

MULLAYA

"Addada," "Nadiba," or "Naddaba" in classical Arabic. Traditionally, a *mullaya* is a woman hired to lead call-and-response with women mourning at funerals. She is considered very good if she can bring the women to a crying frenzy with her improvised heartbreaking verses about the dead.

NAMMU

The first deity recorded in Sumerian mythology (ca. 4000 B.C.), she is the mother of all creation who gave birth to heaven and earth. She is represented by the sea.

NANNA
Granny.

PALESTINE HOTEL
A major hotel in Baghdad where many foreign journalists and news organizations were based during the 2003 war. It overlooks al-Firdaws Square where the famous toppling of Saddam's statue took place.

QURNA
See Eridu, Qurna, Ur.

RASHID HOTEL
A five-star landmark hotel in Baghdad. After the 1991 Gulf War, a mosaic of the American president George H. W. Bush was placed in the lobby of the Rashid Hotel in central Baghdad forcing anyone entering the hotel to walk across the mosaic. The sole of the shoe is considered unclean in Middle Eastern cultures, and the act of walking on the mosaic was seen as an insult to George Bush. When American troops took the city in the 2003 invasion of Iraq, the mosaic was replaced with a picture of Saddam Hussein.

SABAH
A girl's name meaning "morning."

SAMMURA
An endearing form of the name Samira, which means a "good companion" or "conversation partner."

SHAHRAZAD
Also spelled "Scheherazade," the Persian name of the main narrator and heroine in *One Thousand and One Nights* who saved herself and the women of her country from death at the hands of King Shahryar by weaving a compelling story night after night for one thousand and one nights.

SHAHRYAR

Name of the king in *One Thousand and One Nights* who would wed a virgin each night and then kill her the next morning to assure she would never betray him with another man.

SHATT AL-ARAB

The point of confluence of the Euphrates and Tigris in the town of Qurna in southern Iraq, Shatt al-Arab means "stream of the Arabs." It ends in the Gulf and its banks are lined with thickets of palm trees. It is one of the possible sites of the Garden of Eden.

SHEIKH

The elder of a tribe.

SHI`A

A follower of prophet Muhammad and his successors (the twelve imams), the first being Ali. The term "Shi`a" means "group" or "followers" and originally referred to the followers of Ali. Because the Shi`a believe the rightful succession to the prophet Muhammad was through the family line, they followed Ali the Prophet's son-in-law and cousin. When Ali was assassinated in 661, the larger Muslim population began to splinter. Hussein, Ali's son, eventually led a rebellion in Kerbala, Iraq, in the year 680. He was slaughtered brutally and his death is marked as a foundational moment for the Shi`a sect and is celebrated each year during the month of Ashura. The festival is marked by pilgrimage and symbols of martyrdom including people enacting passion plays and beating and whipping themselves in commemoration of Hussein's suffering and murder. Shi`as constitute the second largest sect in Islam.

SHLONICH

"How are you?" in Iraqi dialect. Literally translates as "what color are you?"

SUNNI

A member of the largest denomination of Islam. After the prophet Muhammad's death the Sunnis followed Muhammad's companion, Abu Bakr, who
became the first caliph after Muhammad. As opposed to the Shi`a, who be-
lieve that the ruler of the Muslim community must be a descendant of the
Prophet and his family, the Sunnis believe in the consensus of the community and that the initial succession of Abu Bakr after Muhammad's death was
legitimate. Sunni Muslims constitute eighty to ninety percent of the global
Muslim population.

TA`AL
Come here.

TIS`AH
Nine.

UMM
Mother of.

UR
See Eridu, Qurna, Ur.

WAYN ALLAH?
Where is God?

THE WELL
In the Mullaya's final speech she references text taken from the following
Iraqi song:

> When you drink water out of a well
> Beware of throwing a stone into it!
> Surely, one day you'll come back
> To quench your thirst there
> Beware of throwing a stone into it.

You will return to the well one day
Thirsty and assured that it will be there
But you will not find anything; neither spring, nor river
So beware of throwing a stone into it.

Life is treacherous
So think, time and again!
Tend to your affairs discreetly
It's better; you keep trouble at bay
Beware of throwing a stone into it!
Listen to me! You may benefit!
Take note and learn!
You may desire benefit for yourself
But remember to be fair to fellow humans!
Beware of throwing a stone into it!

—"The Well," composition and text by Hassan Khewka,
translation by Sinan Antoon

YABOO
A cry of disaster or tragedy.

YA`NI
I mean.

MULLAYA
"this river is the color of worn soles"

MULLAYA
"bring me back the water I was created in"

LAYAL

"death is only teasing me"

LAYAL

"she is the branch's blossom"

Transition from LAYAL *to* AMAL

HUDA

"anybody who was intelligent was Communist"

IRAQI GIRL *dancing to N'Sync*

Transition into UMM GHADA

Transition into THE AMERICAN

MULLAYA
"hear my voice"

MULLAYA *transitioning into* NANNA
"you like to buy?"

NANNA
"two dollar?"

Set design by Antje Ellermann for the Geffen Theater, Los Angeles

Set design by Antje Ellermann for Seattle Repertory Theatre

ABOUT THE PLAYWRIGHT

As the actor and playwright of *9 Parts of Desire,* Heather Raffo received a 2005 Susan Smith Blackburn Prize Special Commendation, the Marian Seldes–Garson Kanin Fellowship, and a 2005 Lucille Lortel Award for best solo show as well as an Outer Critics Circle nomination and a Drama League nomination for distinguished performance. This is Raffo's first work as a playwright; she trained as an actress and has spent the last six years performing professionally off Broadway, off West End, on national tours, in regional theater, and in film. Raffo received her bachelor of arts in English from the University of Michigan, and her master of fine arts in acting performance from the University of San Diego at the Old Globe Theater. She has also studied at the Royal Academy of Dramatic Art in London. Born in Michigan, Raffo now lives in New York. Her father is originally from Iraq, and her mother is American.